If Not You, Who? If Not Now, When?
written by Dr. Ken Smith & Bishop Dominic Luque
1st Edition © 2025 Marketplace Network
ISBN: 979-8-234-02449-7

If Not You, Who? If Not Now, When?

We dedicate this book to every believer who has ever felt the pull of purpose, the weight of responsibility, or the quiet whisper of God calling them into something more.

Between us, we carry more than forty-five years of working for the Lord — years marked by victories, valleys, breakthroughs, mistakes, miracles, and the kind of growth that only comes through time, surrender, and obedience. We have served in different places, different seasons, and different capacities, but one truth has remained constant: God is faithful to finish what He starts.

We dedicate this work to the sons and daughters who are rising, to the leaders being shaped in hidden places, to the servants who have remained faithful when no one was watching, and to the ones who are just beginning to discover who they truly are in Christ.

We dedicate it to those who mentored us, corrected us, believed in us, and refused to let us settle for less than what God placed inside us. Their fingerprints are on every chapter.

And we dedicate it to you — the reader — because if this book is in your hands, it means God is stirring something in your life. Something real. Something intentional. Something worth building.

May these pages strengthen your faith, clarify your calling, and remind you that your life carries weight, purpose, and eternal impact.

With honor, gratitude, and expectation,

Dr. Ken & Bishop Dominic – Marketplace Network

TABLE OF CONTENTS

CHAPTER 1

The Call to Ministry: Hearing God's Invitation

The call to ministry rarely arrives with fanfare. It does not always come through visions, dreams, or dramatic encounters. More often, it begins as a quiet stirring — a sense that God is drawing you toward something deeper, something greater, something beyond your current understanding. Ministry begins with an invitation, not an announcement.

Every believer is called to ministry. Not necessarily to a pulpit, a platform, or a title, but to a life of service, influence, and spiritual impact. Ministry is not a position; it is a posture. It is the willingness to say, "Here I am, Lord. Use me." It is the readiness to respond when God speaks, even when the path is unclear.

The call of God is deeply personal. It is shaped by your story, your gifts, your experiences, and your identity. God does not call you to be someone else; He calls you to be the fullest version of who He created you to be. Your calling is not a copy — it is an original assignment designed specifically for you.

Throughout Scripture, God called ordinary people to extraordinary purposes. Moses was tending sheep when

God called him. David was watching over his father's flock. Gideon was hiding in fear. Peter was fishing. Matthew was collecting taxes. None of them were seeking ministry, yet ministry found them. God often calls people in the middle of their everyday lives.

The call to ministry begins with hearing God's voice. Not audibly, necessarily, but internally — through Scripture, through prayer, through conviction, through circumstances, and through the gentle prompting of the Holy Spirit. Jesus said in

John 10:27, "My sheep hear My voice."

Hearing God is not a rare gift; it is a natural part of relationship with Him.

But hearing is only the beginning. The call requires response. When God speaks, you must answer. When God stirs your heart, you must move. When God opens a door, you must walk through it. Delayed obedience is often the greatest enemy of calling. The longer you wait, the harder it becomes to step forward.

The call to ministry also requires surrender. You cannot hold on to your own plans and fully embrace God's. You cannot cling to comfort and step into purpose. You cannot follow Christ and remain unchanged. Ministry requires letting go — of fear, of excuses, of limitations, of the need for control. Surrender is not loss; it is alignment.

The call to ministry is not always convenient. It may disrupt your plans, challenge your assumptions, and stretch your faith. But it will also awaken your purpose, deepen your relationship with God, and transform your life. Ministry is not a burden; it is a privilege. It is the honor of partnering with God in His work on earth.

I want to speak directly into your journey. Hear this thought, inspired by the Word of the Lord - If Not You, Who? If you do not respond to God's call, who will reach the people assigned to you? Who will speak the words only you can speak? Who will carry the compassion only you carry? Who will step into the spaces God designed for you?

Your call is not accidental. Your gifts are not random. Your story is not wasted. Your life is not ordinary. Hear the Word of the Lord: If Not Now, When? When will you say yes? When will you step forward? When will you trust God with your future? When will you embrace the purpose He has placed within you?

The call to ministry is not for later. It is for now. God is speaking. God is calling. God is inviting you into something greater. Your task is to respond.

The Call to Ministry

Let me talk to you in a straightforward way for a moment. When someone begins to sense that God may be drawing them toward ministry, the first reaction is rarely confidence. It's usually hesitation. Not because they don't love God, but because they're not sure what He sees in them. If that's where you are, you're not alone. Most people who eventually step into ministry start from the same place.

You might feel unprepared. You might feel unworthy. You might be carrying disappointment from past leadership. Or maybe you simply don't see yourself as "that kind of person." But here's the truth: the very fact that you're wrestling with these thoughts means something is already alive in you. People who aren't being drawn don't wrestle like this. They don't think this deeply about purpose. They don't feel this kind of pull.

So instead of trying to decide whether you're "ready," pay attention to what's waking up in you. Something is shifting—maybe quietly, maybe slowly—but it's shifting. And that shift matters. It's the early sign that God is preparing you for something more than where you've been.

You don't need a title. You don't need a platform. You don't need perfect clarity. What you need is honesty— honesty about what's stirring in you, honesty about what you're sensing, honesty about the fact that something in you is responding to God even if you don't fully understand it yet.

Let this settle in your heart: you're not behind, and you're not disqualified. You're being invited. Invitations from God rarely come when we feel prepared. They come when He knows it's time and before you move on, take a moment to picture your own path. If you were to honor what's stirring in you right now, where could you realistically see yourself in six months when it comes to recognizing and responding to God's call? And if you continued to grow in courage and clarity, where could you see yourself in one year in terms of stepping into ministry with confidence and purpose? Take this page to write some notes on this as you are led by the prompting of the Holy Spirit.

Where do you see yourself in 6 months as it relates to this chapter's theme?

Where do you see yourself in 1 year as it relates to this chapter's theme?

CHAPTER 2

Understanding Your Destiny and Spiritual Identity

Every calling begins with identity. Before God sends you, He establishes who you are. Before He entrusts you with influence, He anchors you in identity. Destiny is not discovered through ambition; it is revealed through relationships.

Identity is the foundation of destiny. If you do not know who you are, you will never understand what you are called to do. If you do not know who God created you to be, you will spend your life trying to become someone else.

Scripture teaches that you are fearfully and wonderfully made. You are chosen, appointed, anointed, and set apart. You are not an accident. You are not a mistake. You are not a random combination of traits and experiences. You are intentionally designed for a purpose.

Identity is not shaped by culture, circumstances, or opinions. It is shaped by God. When you anchor your identity in Him, you become unshakable. When you anchor your identity in anything else, you become unstable.

Destiny is the expression of identity. It is the outward manifestation of the inward truth of who you are. Destiny is not something you chase; it is something you grow into. It unfolds as you walk with God, obey His voice, and align your life with His purpose.

Identity protects destiny. When you know who you are, you are not swayed by comparison, insecurity, or fear. You do not compete with others because you understand that your calling is unique. You do not shrink back because you understand that your assignment matters.

Identity also clarifies destiny. When you understand your gifts, passions, and spiritual wiring, you begin to recognize the areas where God is calling you to serve. You begin to see patterns, opportunities, and open doors that align with your purpose.

Identity is not static; it grows as you grow. The more you walk with God, the more He reveals. The more you obey, the more He entrusts. The more you surrender, the more He shapes you.

I want to speak directly into your journey. If Not You, Who? If you do not embrace your identity, who will step into the calling tied to your name? If you do not recognize your worth, who will walk in the authority God gave you?

If you do not accept who God says you are, who will fulfill the assignment designed for you? If Not Now, When? When will you stop doubting your identity? When will you stop comparing yourself to others? When will you start walking in the truth of who God created you to be? Identity is not a future revelation. It is a present reality. Walk in it.

Understanding Your Destiny and Spiritual Identity

A lot of people struggle with destiny because they're still unsure about identity. And if that's where you are, you're not alone. Most believers don't wrestle with purpose because they lack calling—they wrestle because they're not convinced of who they are. When identity feels shaky, destiny feels unreachable. But the truth is, the questions you're asking about your future are actually signs that something deeper is waking up in you.

You may have spent years trying to fit into roles that never felt right. You may have been shaped by other people's expectations or wounded by voices that told you who you weren't. You may have compared yourself to others and assumed they were more qualified, more gifted, or more "chosen." But identity doesn't come from comparison. It comes from God. And when He speaks identity over you, He's not describing who you might become someday—He's revealing who you already are.

Destiny isn't a reward for the confident. It's the natural expression of someone who finally agrees with the truth about themselves. You don't chase destiny; you grow into it. Growth begins the moment you stop trying to be someone else and start accepting who God designed you to be. That acceptance is not arrogance, it's alignment. It's the moment you stop fighting your own design and start cooperating with it.

So let me speak to you as a mentor would: you don't need to have every detail of your future figured out. You don't need to know the full picture. What you need is the courage to acknowledge that God didn't make a mistake when He made you. Identity is the doorway. Destiny is what waits on the other side. The only thing standing between the two is your willingness to believe that what God says about you is actually true, and before you move on, take a moment to picture your own growth. If you allowed God to settle your identity in the next season, where could you realistically see yourself in six months when it comes to embracing who He says you are? If you continued to walk in that clarity, where could you see yourself in one year in terms of stepping into the destiny that flows from a secure identity?

Where do you see yourself in 6 months as it relates to this chapter's theme?

Where do you see yourself in 1 year as it relates to this chapter's theme?

CHAPTER 3

Mentorship: The Missing Link in Spiritual Growth

Every calling needs cultivation. Every destiny needs development. Every believer needs guidance. Mentorship is one of the most overlooked but essential components of spiritual growth.

God designed the kingdom to function through relationships. Moses had Jethro. Joshua had Moses. Elisha had Elijah. Timothy had Paul. The disciples had Jesus. No one grows alone.

Mentorship accelerates growth. It shortens learning curves. It provides wisdom, correction, encouragement, and accountability. A mentor sees what you cannot see, says what you need to hear, and helps you avoid mistakes that could delay your destiny.

Mentorship is not about control; it is about cultivation. A true mentor does not shape you into their image; they help you become who God created you to be. They do not impose their calling on you; they help you discover yours.

Mentorship requires humility. You must be willing to learn, to listen, to receive correction, and to grow. Pride resists mentorship. Humility embraces it.

Mentorship also requires discernment. Not everyone is called to speak into your life. You must choose mentors who carry wisdom, integrity, and spiritual maturity. You must choose people who live what they teach.

Mentorship is not optional. It is essential. Without mentorship, you may grow, but you will grow slowly. With mentorship, you grow with clarity, confidence, and direction. Right here and right now is the crossroads: If Not You, Who? If you do not seek mentorship, who will guide you into the fullness of your calling? If you do not allow others to speak into your life, who will help you avoid unnecessary detours? If you do not pursue growth, who will step into the assignment God has for you? If Not Now, When? When will you seek guidance? When will you pursue growth intentionally? When will you allow God to shape you through the voices He sends? Mentorship is not a sign of weakness. It is a sign of wisdom.

Mentorship: The Missing Link in Spiritual Growth

A lot of people underestimate how much their growth depends on the voices they allow into their lives. Some try to grow alone because they've been disappointed before. Others don't want to feel dependent on anyone. Some simply don't know where to find someone they can trust. If any of those sounds familiar, you're not the only one. Most believers struggle with mentorship long before they ever benefit from it.

You may have been overlooked. You may have been mishandled. You may have been taught to stay quiet, stay small, or stay out of the way. Or maybe you've never had someone take the time to see what's in you. But here's the truth: growth accelerates when someone who has walked the road before you helps you navigate your own. Not to control you. Not to shape you into their image. But to help you recognize what God has already placed in you.

A good mentor doesn't replace your relationship with God—they strengthen it. They don't take over your decisions—they help you make better ones. They don't demand loyalty, they cultivate maturity. If you can honestly say that you've been hesitant to trust again, that hesitation doesn't disqualify you. It just means you've lived enough life to know the difference between guidance and manipulation. That awareness is wisdom, not weakness.

So let me speak to you plainly: you don't need to have the perfect mentor lined up to take this seriously. What you need is openness—openness to learn, openness to grow, openness to let someone speak into your life in a way that brings clarity instead of confusion. Mentorship isn't a sign of immaturity; it's a sign of readiness. It means you're willing to grow on purpose instead of by accident. Before you move on, take a moment to picture your own development. If you allowed yourself to embrace healthy mentorship, where could you realistically see your spiritual growth in six months? And if you continued to walk with humility and openness, where could you see yourself in one year in terms of confidence, maturity, and the kind of person you're becoming under wise guidance?

Where do you see yourself in 6 months as it relates to this chapter's theme?

Where do you see yourself in 1 year as it relates to this chapter's theme?

CHAPTER 4

Faith as the Foundation of Ministry

Every work of God begins with faith. Not talent, not resources, not opportunity — faith. Faith is the invisible substance that makes the impossible possible. It is the bridge between what God has spoken and what we have yet to see. Without faith, calling remains dormant. Without faith, identity remains theory. Without faith, ministry remains an idea instead of a reality.

Hebrews 11:1 defines faith as:

"the substance of things hoped for, the evidence of things not seen." (KJV)

Faith is not wishful thinking; it is spiritual substance. It is the inner conviction that what God has promised is already true, even before it manifests. Faith sees what the natural eye cannot. Faith hears what the natural ear misses. Faith steps where the natural mind hesitates.

Abraham is the model of this kind of faith. God told him to leave his home and go to a land he had never seen. He obeyed without knowing the destination because he trusted the One who called him. His faith was not rooted in clarity; it was rooted in confidence — confidence in God's character, God's promise, and God's timing.

Abraham's obedience teaches us that faith is not about understanding every detail; it is about trusting God enough to take the next step.

Faith is also the antidote to worry. Jesus said in Matthew 6 not to "take thought" — not to allow anxious thoughts to dominate our minds. Worry is not harmless; it is a form of meditation on the wrong thing. It shifts our focus from God's promise to our problem. It moves us from the spiritual realm into the natural one, where the enemy has more influence. Worry is not just unproductive; it is spiritually dangerous because it replaces trust with fear.

Philippians 4:13 reminds us that God supplies all things:

13 Christ is the one who gives me the strength I need to do whatever I must do. (ERV)

When we worry, we step out of alignment with that truth. When we trust, we step back into the flow of God's provision. Faith is not denial of reality; it is recognition of a greater reality — the reality of God's faithfulness.

Faith also requires peace and joy. These are not optional emotions; they are indicators of spiritual alignment. When peace leaves, it is often a sign that we have stepped out of faith and into fear. When joy fades, it is often a sign that we are carrying burdens God never asked us to carry. Peace and joy are not the result of circumstances; they are the fruit of trust. They reveal where our confidence truly lies.

Faith is strengthened through the Word. Romans teaches that faith comes by hearing, and hearing by the

Word of God. The more we immerse ourselves in Scripture, the more our faith grows. The Word reveals God's character, His promises, His patterns, and His ways. It anchors us when life becomes uncertain. It steadies us when emotions fluctuate. It strengthens us when circumstances challenge our belief.

Faith is also strengthened through obedience. Every act of obedience builds spiritual muscle. Every step taken in faith makes the next step easier. Faith grows through use. It is not a static quality; it is a dynamic one. The more you exercise it, the stronger it becomes.

Faith is also strengthened through praise. Praise shifts our focus from our limitations to God's greatness. It reminds us of His power, His goodness, and His faithfulness. Praise is not just worship; it is warfare. It moves us from the natural realm into the spiritual one. It silences the voice of fear and amplifies the voice of God. Praise is one of the most powerful expressions of faith because it declares victory before the battle is won.

Faith is also strengthened through testimony. When we remember what God has done, we gain confidence for what He will do. Testimony is not nostalgia; it is fuel. It reminds us that the God who delivered us before will deliver us again. It reminds us that the God who provided in the past will provide in the future. Testimony turns memory into momentum.

Faith is also strengthened through community. We were never meant to walk alone. When we surround ourselves with believers who speak life, who encourage us, who pray with us, and who stand with us, our faith grows.

Community protects us from isolation, discouragement, and spiritual fatigue. It reminds us that we are part of something larger than ourselves.

Faith is also strengthened through action. James teaches that faith without works is dead. Faith is not passive; it is active. It moves. It speaks. It obeys. It steps out. It takes risks. It refuses to settle. It refuses to shrink back. Faith is not proven by what we believe internally, but by what we do externally. Action is the evidence of belief.

Is your faith on a sure foundation? You need to use the faith you have to make the difference. If Not You, Who? If you do not step out in faith, who will reach the people assigned to you? Who will pray the prayers only you can pray? Who will speak the words only you can speak? Who will carry the compassion only you carry? If Not Now, When? Now is the appointed time to be a blessing in someone's life. Faith is not something you wait to use. Faith is something you activate now. Delay weakens faith. Obedience strengthens it. The longer you wait to step into your calling, the harder it becomes. The longer you postpone obedience, the more opportunities pass by. Faith is not built in hesitation; it is built in action. Faith is the foundation of ministry because ministry requires trust.

Trust in God's voice. Trust in God's timing. Trust in God's provision. Trust in God's power. Trust in God's plan. Without faith, ministry becomes a burden. With faith, ministry becomes a joy. Faith is not the absence of fear; it is the decision to move forward despite fear. It is the choice to believe God more than your circumstances.

It is the choice to trust His promise more than your doubts. It is the choice to step out even when you cannot see the whole path. Faith is the foundation because faith is the beginning. Faith is the beginning because God is calling you — now!

Faith as the Foundation of Ministry

A lot of people misunderstand faith because they think it's supposed to feel strong, loud, or dramatic. But most of the time, faith begins quietly. It starts as a small conviction that refuses to go away, even when you can't explain it. If you've ever felt that kind of pull—the kind that doesn't match your resources, your confidence, or your circumstances—that's usually the sign that God is inviting you into something bigger than your comfort zone.

You may be the kind of person who wants clarity before you move. You may want details, timelines, or guarantees. You may want to know the "how" before you say yes to the "what." But faith rarely works that way. Faith grows when you take the step you can see, not the one you wish you could. If you've been waiting for everything to make sense before you move, you're going to stay stuck longer than God intends.

Faith isn't about pretending you're fearless. It's about trusting God enough to move even when you still feel unsure. It's about taking the next step without demanding the whole map. It's about believing that God is already in the place He's asking you to go. If you've been wrestling with doubt, hesitation, or the fear of making a mistake, that doesn't mean you lack faith, it means you're human. Faith isn't the absence of fear; it's the decision to move anyway.

So let me speak to you plainly: you don't need perfect confidence to walk in faith. You don't need to feel bold every day. You don't need to have the same level of certainty as the people you admire. What you need is the willingness to trust that God knows what He's doing with your life, even when you don't. Faith is not about understanding every detail—it's about trusting the One who does. Before you turn the page, take a moment to picture your own journey. If you allowed yourself to take one real step of faith in this area, where could you see yourself in six months when it comes to trusting God with the parts of ministry that feel uncertain? If you continued to walk in that trust, where could you see yourself in one year in terms of confidence, obedience, and the kind of faith that actually moves you forward? Take a few moments of sober reflection on these two questions and jot down some notes on your faith trajectory this year!

Where do you see yourself in 6 months as it relates to this chapter's theme?

Where do you see yourself in 1 year as it relates to this chapter's theme?

•

CHAPTER 5

Hearing God: The Still, Small Voice

Hearing God is the most essential skill in ministry. It is the difference between striving and flowing, between guessing and knowing, between reacting to life and responding to God. Ministry does not begin with activity; it begins with listening. Before God sends you, He speaks to you. Before He uses you, He guides you. Before He entrusts you with influence, He teaches you how to hear His voice.

Many believers struggle with this because they expect God to speak loudly, dramatically, or unmistakably. But Scripture paints a different picture. When Elijah stood on the mountain waiting for God to speak, he encountered a wind so strong it tore the rocks apart, but God was not in the wind. Then came an earthquake, but God was not in the earthquake. Then came a fire, but God was not in the fire. Finally, Elijah heard "a still, small voice" (1 Kings 19:11–12):

11 Then the Lord said to Elijah, "Go, stand in front of me on the mountain. I, the Lord, will pass by you." Then a very strong wind blew. The wind caused the mountains to break apart. It broke large rocks in front of the Lord. But that wind was not the Lord. After that wind, there was an earthquake. But that earthquake was not the Lord. 12 After the earthquake, there was a fire. But that fire was not the Lord. After the fire, there was a quiet, gentle voice.

That is where God was. God often speaks quietly because He wants relationship, not reaction. He wants your attention, not your adrenaline. He wants you to lean in, to listen, to quiet your heart enough to recognize His whisper. The still, small voice is not a sign of God's distance; it is a sign of His closeness. He whispers because He is near.

Learning to hear God begins with learning to quiet the noise. The world is loud. Our thoughts are loud. Our fears are loud. Our schedules are loud. But God does not compete with noise; He waits for stillness. This is why Jesus often withdrew to solitary places to pray. He understood that clarity requires quiet. If the Son of God needed stillness to hear the Father, how much more do we?

Jesus also taught us that the enemy attacks through the mind. In Matthew 6, He warned us not to "take thought" — not to allow anxious thoughts to dominate our thinking. The enemy speaks through fear, doubt, confusion, and distraction. God speaks through peace, clarity, conviction, and alignment. One voice agitates; the other settles. One voice pressures; the other invites. One voice condemns; the other corrects. Learning to hear God requires learning to recognize the difference.

Scripture is the foundation for hearing God. God will never contradict His Word. The more you immerse yourself in Scripture, the more familiar you become with God's tone, His patterns, His priorities, and His ways. When Jesus confronted the enemy in the wilderness, He did not rely on emotion or instinct. He responded with Scripture: "It is written" (Luke 4:4). The Word anchored Him. The Word guided Him. The Word protected Him. The Word is still the clearest way God speaks.

Hearing God also requires purity of heart. 1 John 1:9 teaches that when we confess our sins, God is faithful to forgive us. Sin does not remove God's voice, but it distorts our ability to hear it. It creates static. It clouds discernment. It dulls sensitivity. Repentance clears the frequency. It restores clarity. It reopens the channel of communication. Purity is not about perfection; it is about alignment.

Hearing God also requires sensitivity to the Holy Spirit. Jesus said the Spirit would guide us into all truth. The Spirit speaks through impressions, promptings, convictions, and inner knowing. Many believers expect God's voice to sound external, but most often it sounds internal — a thought that carries peace, a prompting that carries weight, a conviction that carries clarity. The Spirit speaks from within because He lives within.

This is why Jesus described the Spirit's voice as something that rises from the inner man. Many believers describe it as a gentle nudge, a quiet thought, or a sense of direction that feels deeper than emotion. It is like a whisper in the non-dominant ear — subtle, but unmistakable once you learn to recognize it. God does not shout over the noise; He invites you to tune in. Hearing God also requires wise counsel.

Hearing God: The Still, Small Voice

A lot of people struggle with hearing God because they expect His voice to sound like their expectations—loud, dramatic, unmistakable. And when it doesn't, they assume something is wrong with them. But most of the time, God speaks in ways that require attention, not adrenaline. If you've ever felt a quiet nudge, a gentle thought that didn't come from pressure or fear, or a subtle pull toward something good and right—that's often where His voice begins.

You might be the kind of person who wants God to speak in a way that removes all doubt. You might wish He would make things obvious, so you don't risk getting it wrong. Or maybe you've been in environments where people made hearing God sound complicated or mystical. But hearing Him isn't about volume—it's about relationship. God doesn't shout to compete with the noise around you; He speaks in a way that invites you to slow down and pay attention.

If you've ever wondered whether God speaks to you at all, consider this: the very desire to hear Him is already evidence that He's drawing you. People who aren't being invited don't feel that pull. And if you've been afraid of mistaking your own thoughts for His, that fear doesn't disqualify you—it simply means you care about honoring Him. That's a good sign. It means your heart is already leaning in the right direction.

So let me speak to you plainly: hearing God is less about trying harder and more about becoming quieter. It's about giving Him space in your thoughts, not demanding a certain style of communication. It's about trusting that He knows how to speak to you in a way you'll understand, even if it's softer than you expected. And the more you practice listening, the more familiar His voice becomes. And before you move forward, take a moment to picture your own growth in this area. If you allowed yourself to slow down and listen with intention, where could you realistically see yourself in six months when it comes to recognizing God's voice in the quiet moments? And if you continued to grow in sensitivity and confidence, where could you see yourself in one year in terms of hearing Him clearly enough to guide your decisions and your ministry?

Where do you see yourself in 6 months as it relates to this chapter's theme?

Where do you see yourself in 1 year as it relates to this chapter's theme?

CHAPTER 6

Power of Praise and the Presence of God

Praise is one of the most underestimated spiritual forces in the life of a believer. Many see praise as something we do before a sermon, or as a musical expression reserved for Sunday mornings. But Scripture reveals something far deeper: praise is a spiritual weapon, a doorway into God's presence, and a catalyst for breakthrough. Praise is not just worship — it is warfare. It is not just gratitude — it is alignment. It is not just expression — it is activation.

God designed praise to shift atmospheres. Not just the atmosphere around you, but the atmosphere within you. Praise recalibrates your heart, refocuses your mind, and repositions your spirit. It lifts your attention from the natural realm into the spiritual one. It silences fear, weakens doubt, and strengthens faith. Praise is not something you do when you feel good; it is something you do because God is good.

Scripture tells us that God "inhabits the praises of His people." That means praise creates a dwelling place for God's presence. When you praise, you are not just singing

— you are building a sanctuary. You are creating a space where God's presence becomes tangible, where His voice becomes clearer, and where His power becomes active. Praise is not a warmup; it is an entry point.

This is why the Psalms are filled with commands to praise. David understood that praise was not optional; it was essential. He praised God in victory and in distress, in clarity and in confusion, in strength and in weakness. Praise was not his reaction to circumstances; it was his response to God. When he felt overwhelmed, he praised. When he felt discouraged, he praised. When he felt attacked, he praised. Praise was his way of staying aligned with God's presence.

If you struggle to praise, Scripture gives you a starting point. Read the Psalms. Read them aloud. Read them with intention. Read them until your heart begins to shift. Praise is not always natural at first, especially when life feels heavy. But the more you practice it, the more it becomes a rhythm — a spiritual reflex that strengthens your faith.

Praise also moves you into the Spirit. Jude 1:3 teaches us to "contend for the faith," and praise is one of the ways we contend. It pulls us out of the mental realm — where the enemy attacks — and into the spiritual realm, where God reigns. Praise lifts us above our circumstances and places us in the atmosphere of God's authority. It is difficult for fear to survive in an atmosphere of praise. It is difficult for doubt to speak when praise is loud. It is difficult for discouragement to linger when praise is active.

Praise also prepares the heart to receive the Word. James 1:21 teaches that the Word becomes "engrafted" into us — it becomes part of who we are:

21 So get rid of everything evil in your lives—every kind of wrong you do. Be humble and accept God's teaching that is planted in your hearts. This teaching can save you. (ERV)

Praise softens the soil of the heart so the Word can take root. It clears away distraction, breaks up hardness, and opens us to revelation. Praise is not just emotional; it is spiritual preparation.

Praise also strengthens faith. Hebrews 11:1 teaches that faith is the substance of things hoped for. Praise reminds us of what God has done, which strengthens our belief in what He will do. Praise is a declaration of trust. It says, "God, I believe You even before I see the answer." Praise is faith expressed. It is confidence vocalized. It is hope made audible.

Praise also silences the enemy. When Jesus confronted the enemy in the wilderness, He responded with Scripture, but He also lived a life of praise. Praise is a declaration of God's supremacy. It reminds the enemy that he is defeated. It reminds your spirit that God is victorious. It reminds your mind that God is faithful. Praise is not passive; it is powerful.

Praise also brings clarity. When you praise, the noise of life begins to fade. The voice of fear grows quiet. The voice of God grows clear. Praise tunes your heart to God's frequency. It helps you hear the still, small voice described in 1 Kings 19:11–12. Praise is not just expression; it is alignment.

Hear my heart, If you do not cultivate a life of praise, who will shift the atmosphere in your home? Who will bring God's presence into your workplace? Who will carry the sound of faith into environments filled with fear? Who will model a life anchored in God's goodness?

If We Don't Praise Him Now, Then When? Praise is not something you wait to practice. It is something you activate now. Praise is not something you save for Sunday. It is something you carry into every day. Praise is not something you postpone until life improves. It is something you use to transform your life now. Praise is the doorway to God's presence. Praise is the weapon that defeats discouragement. Praise is the language of faith. Praise is the atmosphere of breakthrough. Praise is the sound of a believer who knows God is near.

If you want to walk in your calling, cultivate praise. If you want to hear God clearly, cultivate praise. If you want to strengthen your faith, cultivate praise. If you want to shift your environment, cultivate praise. Praise is not just what you do — it is who you become. A person who carries the presence of God. A person who walks in faith. A person who changes atmospheres. A person who responds to God with trust, gratitude, and expectation. Praise is your power. Use it. Live in it. Let it shape you.

The Power of Praise and the Presence of God

A lot of believers underestimate what praise actually does inside them. They think of it as music, or as something that happens during a service, or as a warm-up before the "real" part of church begins. But praise is far more personal than that. It's the way your spirit shifts its focus. It's the way your heart resets. It's the way your mind stops rehearsing fear and starts remembering who God is. If you've ever felt stuck, heavy, or spiritually disconnected, praise is often the first place where movement begins.

You might be someone who praises easily in church but struggles to do it alone. You might feel awkward praising when no one else is around. Or maybe you've gone through seasons where praise felt forced because your circumstances didn't match the words coming out of your mouth, but praise isn't about pretending everything is fine. It's about choosing to acknowledge God's presence even when your emotions haven't caught up yet. Praise doesn't deny reality — it invites God into it.

There's a reason praise changes the atmosphere. It interrupts the internal noise that fear, doubt, and discouragement create. It pulls your attention away from what's wrong and anchors you in the One who is steady. And when you praise, you're not trying to get God to show up — you're becoming aware that He already has. Praise doesn't manipulate God; it awakens you. It clears the fog. It softens the heart. It makes room for His presence to become tangible again.

So let me mentor you into this plainly: praise is not about personality or musical ability. It's about posture. It's about choosing to lift your attention when everything in you wants to shut down. It's about creating space for God's presence to settle in the places where you've felt overwhelmed or alone. If praise has felt distant or unfamiliar to you, that doesn't mean you're doing it wrong — it simply means you're learning how to let God meet you in a new way. Before you move forward, take a moment to picture your own growth in this area. If you allowed praise to become a consistent part of your daily rhythm, where could you realistically see yourself in six months when it comes to experiencing God's presence in a deeper, more personal way? If you continued to cultivate that posture, where could you see yourself in one year in terms of living with a clearer mind, a stronger spirit, and a heart that responds to God with confidence and freedom?

Where do you see yourself in 6 months as it relates to this chapter's theme?

Where do you see yourself in 1 year as it relates to this chapter's theme?

CHAPTER 7

Miracles: Signs of God's Compassion

Miracles are not merely supernatural events; they are expressions of God's compassion. They reveal His heart, His nearness, and His desire to intervene in the lives of His people. Throughout Scripture, miracles were never performed for spectacle or entertainment. They were demonstrations of God's love, His mercy, and His commitment to restore what was broken. Miracles are not proof of our power; they are proof of His presence.

Jesus made this clear in Matthew 11:23 when He said that if the miracles performed in certain cities had been done in Sodom, the people would have repented and the city would still exist, I'm paraphrasing but let's look at it here:

23 "And you, Capernaum, will you be lifted up to heaven? No! You will be thrown down to the place of death. I did many miracles in you. If these same miracles had happened in Sodom, the people there would have stopped sinning, and it would still be a city today. (ERV)

That statement reveals something profound: miracles are invitations. They call people back to God. They awaken hearts. They soften resistance. They reveal the goodness of God in ways words alone cannot.

Miracles are not rare in Scripture, nor were they rare in the ministry of Jesus. He performed thirty-seven recorded miracles, and thirty-four of them took place in the marketplace — in homes, on roads, in workplaces, and among ordinary people. This tells us something essential: miracles were never meant to be confined to religious settings. They were meant to flow through everyday life. They were meant to meet people where they are.

Miracles are signs of God's compassion. When Jesus healed the sick, fed the hungry, or delivered the oppressed, He was not simply demonstrating power; He was demonstrating love. Scripture often says He was "moved with compassion" before He acted. Compassion is the soil in which miracles grow. When your heart is moved by the suffering of others, you are stepping into the same posture that moved Jesus.

Miracles also reveal the nature of God's kingdom. They show that God is not distant or indifferent. He is active, present, and involved. He cares about physical needs, emotional wounds, relational fractures, and spiritual bondage. Miracles are reminders that God is not limited by circumstances, diagnoses, or impossibilities. They remind us that nothing is too hard for Him.

Miracles also strengthen faith. When you witness God's power, your belief deepens. When you experience His intervention, your confidence grows. When you see Him move in ways that defy explanation, your trust becomes anchored. Miracles are not the foundation of faith, but they are fuel for it. They remind us that the God we serve is alive, powerful, and attentive.

Miracles also open doors for ministry. When people see God move, they become receptive. Hearts soften. Walls come down. Conversations open. Miracles create opportunities to share the love of Christ in ways that words alone cannot. They demonstrate the reality of God's kingdom in tangible form.

But miracles are not random. They follow faith. They follow obedience. They follow compassion. They follow alignment with God's heart. Mark 16:20 teaches that "signs follow those who believe." Miracles are not reserved for apostles, prophets, or pastors. They are available to every believer who walks in faith. The power of God flows through those who trust Him, who listen to Him, and who respond to His leading.

Miracles also require boldness. In Matthew 11:23, as we saw, Jesus made it clear that miracles carry responsibility. When God moves, we must respond. When God speaks, we must obey. When God opens a door, we must walk through it. Miracles are invitations to deeper faith, deeper obedience, and deeper partnership with God.

What about you? If you do not believe for miracles in your sphere, who will? If you do not pray for the sick, who will? If you do not speak life into impossible situations, who will? If you do not carry compassion into broken places, who will? Miracles are not reserved for someone else. They are part of your inheritance as believers. They are part of your calling. They are part of your ministry.

I know what you're going to ask...What if they don't get healed. What if it doesn't happen now? Miracles are not something you wait to believe for. They are something you pursue now. They are something you pray for now. They are something you expect now. The world is hurting now, so we have to believe for the miracle now, not tomorrow. People are desperate now. Needs are overwhelming now. God is ready to move now. The secret: miracles are not about timing; they are about trust. They are not about ability; they are about availability. They are not about your power; they are about His compassion. If you want to walk in the fullness of your calling, cultivate compassion. If you want to see God move, cultivate faith. If you want to experience miracles, cultivate obedience.

Miracles are not distant. They are not rare. They are not reserved. They are the natural expression of a supernatural God working through willing vessels. God is asking you to be one of those vessels.

Miracles: Signs of God's Compassion

A lot of people misunderstand miracles because they focus on the event instead of the heart behind it. They think miracles are about power, spectacle, or spiritual status. But miracles have never been about proving how gifted someone is. They've always been about revealing how deeply God cares. If you've ever wondered why God intervenes the way He does, or why some moments feel marked by His touch while others feel quiet, it's because miracles are expressions of compassion, not performance.

You might be someone who has prayed for miracles and felt disappointed when things didn't happen the way you hoped. You might have seen others experience breakthroughs while you were still waiting. Maybe you've been hesitant to believe for anything supernatural because you don't want to be let down again, but miracles were never meant to be a measure of your worth or your faith level. They are simply moments where God chooses to make His kindness visible.

When Jesus performed miracles, He wasn't trying to impress crowds. He wasn't building a brand. He wasn't proving Himself. He was responding to people — their pain, their hunger, their desperation, their faith, their need. Miracles were His way of saying, "I see you." If you've ever felt unseen, overlooked, or forgotten, that's exactly why this chapter matters. Miracles remind you that God is not distant. He is not indifferent. He is not passive. He is moved by compassion.

So let me speak to you plainly: you don't need to chase miracles to walk with God. You don't need to manufacture moments or try to force something supernatural to happen. What you need is the confidence that God's compassion is already directed toward you. Miracles are not the goal — relationship is. When you understand that, you stop striving for signs and start recognizing the ways God is already present in your life, even in the quiet places. Before you move forward, take a moment to picture your own journey with this. If you allowed yourself to trust God's compassion in a deeper way, where could you realistically see yourself in six months when it comes to believing that His heart is toward you? If you continued to grow in that trust, where could you see yourself in one year in terms of recognizing His presence, expecting His goodness, and walking with a faith that isn't based on spectacle but on relationship? Take some notes here and reflect on these two points as you step into a greater compassion for humanity.

Where do you see yourself in 6 months as it relates to this chapter's theme?

Where do you see yourself in 1 year as it relates to this chapter's theme?

CHAPTER 8

Healing and the Journey of Belief

Healing is one of the clearest expressions of God's heart. From Genesis to Revelation, God reveals Himself as a healer — not occasionally, not reluctantly, but consistently. Healing is not a side ministry or a rare occurrence; it is part of the nature of God. When Jesus walked the earth, He healed the sick, restored the broken, and delivered the oppressed. He did not heal to prove something; He healed because compassion moved Him. Healing is not just an act of power — it is an act of love.

Mark 16:20 teaches that "signs follow those who believe." Healing is not reserved for a select few. It is not limited to pastors, prophets, or evangelists. It is available to every believer who walks in faith. Healing flows through those who trust God, who listen to His voice, and who respond with compassion. Healing is not about your ability; it is about your availability.

But healing is also a journey. It does not always happen instantly. Sometimes healing manifests immediately, and sometimes it unfolds gradually as faith grows. Jesus told the leper in Matthew 8:4;

4 Then Jesus said to him, "Don't tell anyone about what happened. But go and let the priest look at you. [a] And offer the gift that Moses commanded for people who are made well. This will show everyone that you are healed." (ERV)

It was not because the miracle was fragile, but because the process was sacred. Healing often requires privacy, reflection, and confirmation. It is not always meant to be broadcast; sometimes it is meant to be stewarded.

Healing also requires belief. Jesus said in Luke 17:6 that even faith the size of a mustard seed can uproot a mulberry tree. The Greek implies continuous action — "you can keep saying." Healing often requires persistence. It requires speaking God's Word over your body, your mind, and your circumstances. It requires aligning your confession with God's promise. It requires refusing to let fear or doubt take root.

Healing also requires partnership. God provides the power, but we provide the faith. God provides the promise, but we provide the agreement. God provides the miracle, but we provide the obedience. Healing is not passive; it is active. It requires engaging with Scripture, praying with expectation, and speaking with authority. It requires believing that what God has spoken is true, even when symptoms remain.

Healing also requires wisdom. Scripture teaches that healing and confirmation work together. Jesus told the leper to show himself to the priest — not because the priest healed him, but because the priest confirmed what God had done. Today, doctors often play that role. They confirm healing. They provide clarity. They help us steward the miracle. Faith and wisdom are not enemies; they are partners.

Healing also requires compassion. Jesus was moved with compassion before He healed. Compassion opens the door for God's power to flow. When your heart is moved by the suffering of others, you are stepping into the same posture that moved Jesus. Healing is not about demonstrating power; it is about demonstrating love. It is about seeing people the way God sees them — valuable, precious, and worthy of restoration.

Healing also requires peace. Isaiah 26:3 teaches that God keeps in perfect peace:

3 God, you give true peace to people who depend on you, to those who trust in you. (ERV)

Peace is not just an emotion; it is a spiritual position. When you remain in peace, you remain in faith. When you lose peace, you often step into fear. Healing flows in an atmosphere of peace. It thrives where trust is present. It grows where anxiety is silenced.

Healing also requires persistence. The enemy often attacks through symptoms, fear, and discouragement. He tries to convince you that nothing is happening, that God is not moving, that healing is not possible. But Scripture teaches that we walk by faith, not by sight. Healing often begins before it becomes visible. It begins in the spirit before it manifests in the body. It begins with belief before it becomes experience.

And you? Are you fit for the Master's use to bring healing to the world? If you do not believe for healing — for yourself, your family, your community — who will? If you do not pray for the sick, who will? If you do not carry compassion into broken places, who will? If you do not speak life into impossible situations, who will?

Healing is not someone else's assignment. It is part of your calling as a believer. It is part of your ministry. It is part of your identity. Healing is not something you wait to believe in. It is something you pursue now. It is something you pray for now. It is something you expect now. The world is hurting now. People are suffering now. Like with miracles, healing is also not about timing; it is about trust. It is not about ability; it is about availability. It is not about your strength; it is about His compassion. Healing and the Miraculous are interlinked.

If you want to walk in your calling, cultivate belief. If you want to see God move, cultivate compassion. If you want to experience healing, cultivate faith. Healing is not distant. It is not rare. It is not reserved. It is the natural expression of a supernatural God working through willing vessels. And, well, God is asking you to be one of those vessels today!

Healing and the Journey of Belief

A lot of people struggle with healing because they assume it should always happen instantly, dramatically, or in the same way they've seen it happen for others, and when it doesn't, they start questioning themselves, their faith, or whether God even sees them. The truth, healing has never been about performance. It has always been about God's heart. Healing is compassion in motion. It's God responding to pain, not testing your spirituality.

You might be someone who has prayed for healing and felt discouraged when nothing seemed to change. You might have watched others receive breakthrough while you were still waiting. Or maybe you've been afraid to believe again because disappointment left a mark. But healing isn't a formula. It's a journey — one that looks different for every person. Some experience it suddenly. Others experience it gradually, and some discover that the process of believing becomes just as transformative as the healing itself.

When Jesus healed, He wasn't trying to prove a point. He wasn't trying to build a reputation. He wasn't trying to create a spectacle. He healed because compassion moved Him, and that same compassion is directed toward you. Healing isn't reserved for the spiritual elite. It isn't limited to people with titles or platforms. Healing flows through ordinary believers who simply make themselves available — and it flows to those who trust that God's heart is for them, even when the timeline doesn't make sense.

Here's the mentoring moment: healing is not about your ability. It's about your willingness to believe that God is still who He says He is. It's about trusting that He hasn't forgotten you, overlooked you, or changed His mind about you. If your healing has been slow, that doesn't mean it's denied — it means God is walking with you through a process that is shaping your faith as much as it is restoring your body or your heart. Now, take a moment to picture your own journey with this. If you allowed yourself to believe again — even in small, steady ways — where could you realistically see yourself in six months when it comes to trusting God for healing in your life or through your life? And if you continued to grow in that trust, where could you see yourself in one year in terms of confidence, compassion, and the kind of faith that makes room for God to heal in His way and His timing?

Where do you see yourself in 6 months as it relates to this chapter's theme?

Where do you see yourself in 1 year as it relates to this chapter's theme?

CHAPTER 9

Marketplace Ministry: Where Faith Meets Real Life

Marketplace ministry is not a modern idea. It is not a trend, a movement, or a new strategy. It is the original context of ministry. Long before church buildings, livestreams, conferences, or formal services, believers lived out their faith in the rhythms of daily life — in homes, in fields, in shops, in community gatherings, and in the places where people worked, traded, and struggled. Ministry was never meant to be confined to a sanctuary. It was meant to flow through the marketplace.

Jesus Himself modeled this. Out of His thirty-seven recorded miracles, thirty-four took place outside religious settings. They happened in the streets, in homes, on hillsides, in boats, and in the middle of ordinary life. That alone reveals something essential: God moves where people live. He moves where people hurt. He moves where people gather. He moves where people work. Ministry is not limited to pulpits; it is expressed wherever believers carry the presence of Christ.

Only a small percentage of believers are called to formal pulpit ministry. Perhaps one percent is called to media. But the remaining ninety-six percent are called to minister in the marketplace. Not as lesser ministers, but as essential ones. The kingdom of God advances not only through sermons, but through the lives of believers who bring Christ into every sphere of society.

The early church understood this. They met in homes, shared meals, prayed together, and carried the presence of God into their communities. Hebrews 10:25 reminds us:

25 We must not quit meeting together, as some are doing. No, we need to keep on encouraging each other. This becomes more and more important as you see the Day getting closer. (ERV)

Marketplace ministry is not always about preaching or teaching. Sometimes it is expressed through integrity, compassion, generosity, or the way we steward our responsibilities. It is revealed in how we treat coworkers, how we handle pressure, how we respond to conflict, and how we carry ourselves when no one is watching. Ministry is not always a message; often it is a posture.

Integrity is one of the most powerful forms of ministry. People may not understand theology, but they understand honesty. They understand consistency. They understand reliability. When you work with excellence, when you show up on time, when you finish tasks without being asked, when you treat people with respect, you are ministering. You are revealing the character of Christ through your actions.

Compassion is another form of ministry. When you notice someone struggling, when you offer encouragement, when you listen without judgment, when you pray for someone quietly in your heart, you are ministering. Compassion opens doors that sermons cannot. It softens hearts. It builds trust. It reveals the love of God in practical ways.

Marketplace ministry also requires wisdom. Not every moment is the right moment to speak. Not every conversation needs a Scripture. Not every situation requires a spiritual explanation. Jesus said in Matthew 10:16;

16 "Listen! I am sending you, and you will be like sheep among wolves. So be smart like snakes. But also, be like doves and don't hurt anyone. (ERV)

Wisdom helps you discern when to speak and when to listen, when to act and when to wait, when to share and when to simply be present.

Marketplace ministry also requires courage. It takes courage to stand for what is right. It takes courage to maintain integrity when others cut corners. It takes courage to speak hope when negativity dominates. It takes courage to pray for someone when the moment feels uncertain. Courage is not the absence of fear; it is the decision to act despite it.

Marketplace ministry also requires faith. You may not always see immediate results. You may not always receive recognition. You may not always know the impact you are making. But faith reminds you that God is working through you even when you cannot see it. Faith reminds you that your obedience matters. Faith reminds you that your presence carries weight.

Allow me to bring these truths right into your home, If you do not bring Christ into your workplace, who will?

If you do not carry compassion into your environment, who will? If you do not model integrity, who will? If you do not speak hope, who will? You see the importance of why I am saying it like this? This is the correct perspective we must view the hurting and lost with; Marketplace ministry is not someone else's assignment. It is yours. It is part of your identity. It is part of your calling. It is part of your purpose.

The marketplace needs believers now. Your workplace needs light now. Your coworkers need encouragement now. Your environment needs integrity now. Your sphere needs Christ now. Marketplace ministry is not about waiting for the perfect moment. It is about being faithful in the moment you are in. It is about carrying Christ into the places where people need Him most. It is about living your faith in real time, in real situations, with real people.

Why? Because: You are not just employed — you are assigned. You are not just present — you are positioned. You are not just working — you are ministering. The marketplace is your mission field. God has placed you there on purpose.

Marketplace Ministry: Where Faith Meets Real Life

A lot of believers struggle with the idea of ministry because they assume it has to look like a pulpit, a microphone, or a church service, and when their life doesn't fit that mold, they quietly conclude that they must not be "called." Well, Ministry was never meant to be limited to a stage. It was meant to flow through the places where people actually live — workplaces, homes, conversations, routines, and the ordinary spaces where real life happens. If you've ever felt out of place in traditional ministry settings, it may be because your calling was never meant to stay inside a sanctuary.

You might be someone who feels more alive solving problems at work than sitting in a church meeting. You might feel God stirring you in boardrooms, classrooms, studios, or job sites. Maybe you've always sensed that your influence shows up most naturally in everyday interactions — the way you listen, the way you encourage, the way you carry yourself. That's not "less than" ministry. That is ministry. The kingdom advances through people who bring Christ into the spaces where most believers spend the majority of their lives.

Jesus modeled this. Most of His miracles happened in ordinary places — homes, roads, boats, workplaces, and public spaces. He didn't wait for people to come to Him. He met them where they were. And if you've ever wondered why you feel drawn to impact people outside of church walls, it's because God moves where people live, work, gather, and struggle. Marketplace ministry isn't a backup plan. It's the original plan.

More plain talk: you don't need a title to carry God's presence. You don't need a platform to influence people. You don't need a ministry card to make a difference. What you need is the confidence that God can use you right where you are — in your job, your conversations, your relationships, your daily routines. Ministry is not something you step into on Sunday. It's something you carry into every environment you enter. Let's pause and frame this: If you embraced your workplace or daily environment as a place of ministry, where could you realistically see yourself in six months when it comes to living your faith in real, practical ways? If you were to continue to grow in that awareness, where could you see yourself in one year in terms of impact, confidence, and the kind of presence you bring into the spaces where God has already placed you? I know these are deep and tough questions. They are designed that way, so take a few reflective notes and come back to them, to anchor yourself in this as you develop your own marketplace space for ministry and to be a mentor.

Where do you see yourself in 6 months as it relates to this chapter's theme?

Where do you see yourself in 1 year as it relates to this chapter's theme?

CHAPTER 10

Work, Wealth, and the Stewardship of Calling

Work is not a curse. It is not a burden. It is not something God assigned after the fall. Work is part of God's original design. Before sin entered the world, God placed Adam in the garden "to work it and take care of it." Work is sacred. Work is ministry. Work is stewardship. When you understand this, everything about your daily life begins to shift.

Many believers separate their spiritual life from their work life, as if God is only interested in what happens inside a church building. Scripture, however, reveals the opposite. God is deeply invested in how you work, why you work, and what you do with the fruit of your work. Work is not just a means of survival; it is a platform for purpose.

Isaiah 65:23 says that God's people "shall not labor in vain." That means your work is meant to produce something meaningful — not just income, but impact. Not just provision, but purpose. Not just activity, but fruit. When you work with God, your labor becomes part of your calling.

Ecclesiastes 11:1 teaches us to:

"cast your bread upon the waters, for after many days you will find it again." (KJV)

This is a picture of investment, generosity, and long-term stewardship. It reminds us that wealth is not meant to be hoarded; it is meant to be sown. It is meant to circulate. It is meant to bless. Wealth is not the goal — stewardship is.

There is a difference between salary and profit. Salary is what you earn. Profit is what you create. Salary is tied to hours. Profit is tied to value. Salary is limited. Profit has potential. Many believers never step into the fullness of their calling because they only think in terms of salary. God often calls His people to think in terms of stewardship — how to multiply, how to create, how to build, how to bless.

This is not about greed; it is about purpose. Wealth in Scripture is always connected to responsibility. God blesses His people so they can bless others. He provides so they can provide. He increases so they can increase others. Psalm 115:14 says, "May the Lord give you increase, you and your children." Increase is not selfish; it is generational.

Tithing, sowing, and freewill offerings are part of this stewardship. They are not religious rituals; they are spiritual principles. Tithing acknowledges God as the source. Sowing activates faith. Freewill offerings express gratitude. These practices align your heart with God's provision. They remind you that wealth is not your master — God is.

Job 36:11 says,

"If they obey and serve Him, they will spend their days in prosperity and their years in pleasures." (KJV)

Prosperity in Scripture is not merely financial; it is holistic. It includes peace, purpose, relationships, health, and spiritual fulfillment. Prosperity is the fruit of obedience, not the pursuit of wealth. When you follow God's voice, provision follows you.

Work is also a place where character is revealed. Integrity matters. Excellence matters. Diligence matters. When you work with excellence, you honor God. When you work with integrity, you reflect His nature. When you work with diligence, you position yourself for promotion. Scripture teaches that promotion comes from the Lord, but it often flows through the hands of those who notice your faithfulness.

Work is also a place where influence is earned. People watch how you handle pressure, how you respond to conflict, how you treat others, and how you carry yourself. Your work ethic becomes a testimony. Your attitude becomes a ministry. Your consistency becomes a witness. You may never preach a sermon at work, but your life will preach every day.

Wealth is not the goal of calling, but it is often a tool of calling. God uses resources to open doors, fund assignments, support ministries, and bless communities. Wealth in the hands of a believer becomes a weapon — not for selfish gain, but for kingdom impact. When you steward wealth well, you become a conduit of God's generosity.

And you, are you called to steward, to glorify God with your wealth and work? Are you willing to take this mentoring moment and apply it today? If you do not steward your work with excellence, who will? If you do not handle wealth with integrity, who will? If you do not use your resources for kingdom impact, who will? If you do not bring purpose into your workplace, who will?

Let me explain it: Your work is not accidental. Your skills are not random. Your opportunities are not coincidental, they are part of your calling and well, quite simply, now is the time to steward your work with purpose. Now is the time to align your finances with your calling. Now is the time to shift from survival to stewardship. Now is the time to see your workplace as your mission field.

Work is not separate from ministry — it is one of the primary places where ministry happens. Wealth is not separate from calling — it is one of the tools God uses to fulfill it. Stewardship is not optional — it is essential. You are not just working. You are building. You are sowing. You are stewarding. You are ministering. God is with you in every part of it.

Work, Wealth, and the Stewardship of Calling

A lot of believers struggle with the idea of work because they've been taught to see it as something separate from their spiritual life. They think ministry happens in church and work happens everywhere else. And when their job feels ordinary, demanding, or unnoticed, they assume it has little to do with their calling. Work was never meant to be a punishment or a distraction. It was designed by God as a place where purpose is lived out, character is shaped, and influence is expressed.

You might be someone who feels like your job is just a means of survival. You might feel stuck in a role that doesn't look "spiritual." Or maybe you've been waiting for a different opportunity before you take your calling seriously. But calling doesn't begin when circumstances change. It begins when perspective changes. When you start seeing your work as stewardship — not just effort, not just income, not just routine — everything shifts. You begin to realize that God is just as present in your workplace as He is in a sanctuary.

Wealth works the same way. It's not meant to be hoarded, feared, or worshiped. It's meant to be stewarded. It's a tool, not an identity. It's a resource, not a reward. And when you understand that God trusts you with work and wealth because He intends to partner with you, not burden you, you stop separating your spiritual life from your daily life. You begin to see that your calling is woven into the way you show up, the way you serve, the way you create, and the way you handle what God places in your hands.

Consider this mentoring moment: your work matters to God. Your effort matters. Your integrity matters. Your stewardship matters. You don't need a different job to walk in purpose — you need a different lens. When you see your work as part of your calling, you stop waiting for ministry to begin and start realizing it's already happening. When you handle wealth with wisdom and generosity, you step into the kind of influence God can trust. Here's some homework: take a moment to picture your own stewardship. If you embraced your work as part of your calling, where could you realistically see yourself in six months when it comes to purpose, excellence, and the way you show up in your daily responsibilities? If you continued to grow in that mindset, where could you see yourself in one year in terms of influence, financial stewardship, and the confidence that your work and your calling are not separate — they're connected?

Where do you see yourself in 6 months as it relates to this chapter's theme?

Where do you see yourself in 1 year as it relates to this chapter's theme?

•

CHAPTER 11

Excellence, Integrity, and Promotion

Excellence is not perfection. It is not performance. It is not striving. Excellence is the decision to honor God with the best you have in the season you are in. It is the posture of a heart that says, "If I am doing this, I am doing it unto the Lord." Excellence is worship disguised as work. It is ministry expressed through diligence. It is faithfulness made visible.

Integrity is the foundation of excellence. Without integrity, excellence becomes image-management. But with integrity, excellence becomes character. Integrity is of consistency: the same person in private and in public, the same person when watched and when unseen, the same person when praised and when ignored. Integrity is not about reputation; it is about alignment with God's nature.

Promotion in the kingdom is not random. It is not political. It is not based on favoritism. Promotion is the fruit of faithfulness. Psalm 75:6–7 teaches the source of promotion:

6 There is no power on earth that can make a person important. 7 God is the judge. He decides who will be important. He lifts one person up and brings another down. (ERV)

God promotes those who steward well what He has entrusted to them. He elevates those who carry His heart. He advances those who walk in integrity.

Daniel is one of the clearest examples of this. Daniel 6:3 says he had "an excellent spirit," and because of that, the king planned to set him over the entire kingdom. Daniel's excellence was not talent-based; it was character-based. He was faithful, consistent, trustworthy, and disciplined. His excellence made him stand out. His integrity made him unshakable. His faith made him unstoppable.

Excellence is not about being the best; it is about being faithful. It is about doing ordinary things with extraordinary consistency. It is about showing up on time, finishing what you start, honoring your commitments, and treating people with respect. Excellence is not glamorous; it is steady. It is not loud; it is reliable. It is not dramatic; it is consistent.

Integrity is what protects excellence. Without integrity, excellence becomes a performance. But with integrity, excellence becomes a testimony. People may not understand your faith, but they will understand your character. They will notice your honesty. They will respect your consistency. They will trust your word. Integrity builds influence long before you ever speak about God.

Promotion is the result of both. When you walk in excellence and integrity, you position yourself for God's favor. You create an environment where God can trust you with more. You demonstrate that you can handle responsibility, influence, and opportunity. Promotion is not something you chase; it is something you attract through faithfulness.

Joseph is another example. He was promoted to Potiphar's house, put in prison, but eventually was in Pharaoh's palace. His circumstances changed, but his character did not. He worked with excellence whether he was free or imprisoned. He walked in integrity whether he was trusted or falsely accused. His consistency positioned him for elevation. His faithfulness prepared him for influence.

Excellence also creates distinction. In a world where mediocrity is common, excellence stands out. In a culture where shortcuts are normal, integrity shines. People notice when you work with care, when you speak with respect, when you follow through, when you take responsibility, and when you treat others with dignity. Excellence is a form of ministry. Integrity is a form of witness.

Promotion is not always immediate. Sometimes it is delayed. Sometimes it is resisted. Sometimes it is misunderstood. But promotion from God cannot be stopped. When God decides to elevate you, no one can block it. When God opens a door, no one can close it. When God positions you, no one can remove you. Your job is not to force promotion; your job is to remain faithful.

Hear this thought, consider it in your heart, if you do not model excellence in your environment, who will? If you do not walk in integrity, who will? If you do not carry God's character into your workplace, who will? If you do not steward your responsibilities with faithfulness, who will?

You see, your excellence is needed. Your integrity is needed. Your faithfulness is needed. Your influence is needed. You know what I'm going to say, now is the time to raise your standard. Now is the time to walk in integrity. Now is the time to steward your work with excellence. Now is the time to prepare for promotion. Promotion is not a surprise; it is a result. It is the fruit of faithfulness. It is the outcome of consistency. It is the reward of integrity. You are not working for people — you are working for God. You are not building a résumé — you are building a testimony. You are not chasing promotion — you are preparing for it. Excellence positions you. Integrity protects you. Faithfulness promotes you. God is watching every step.

Excellence, Integrity, and Promotion

A lot of people misunderstand excellence because they confuse it with perfection. They think excellence means never making mistakes, never slowing down, never showing weakness. But excellence has never been about performance. It's about posture. It's the quiet decision to honor God with what you have, where you are, even when no one is watching. Excellence is worship disguised as work — but not because the task is spiritual.

You might be someone who has tried to do things well but felt overlooked. You might have watched others get promoted for reasons that had nothing to do with character. Or maybe you've been tempted to cut corners because doing things the right way didn't seem to matter. But integrity is what separates excellence from image management. Integrity is who you are when no one applauds. It's the consistency that keeps your life aligned with God's nature, even when shortcuts look easier.

Promotion in the kingdom doesn't work the way it does in the world. It's not political. It's not random. It's not based on who notices you. Promotion is the fruit of faithfulness — the kind that shows up day after day, even when the work feels unseen. God lifts people who steward well what He places in their hands. He trusts those who carry His heart. And if you've ever wondered whether your diligence matters, this chapter is your reminder that nothing done with integrity is wasted.

The honest truth: you don't need to strive for recognition. You don't need to chase opportunities. You don't need to force doors open. What you need is the confidence that God sees the way you work, the way you serve, the way you carry yourself. Excellence positions you. Integrity sustains you. Promotion comes when God decides the time is right — not when people do. Take a breath and ask yourself this: If I committed to practicing excellence and integrity in a deeper way, where could I realistically see myself in six months when it comes to the quality of my work and the posture of my heart? If I continued to walk that out consistently, where could I see myself in one year in terms of influence, opportunity, and the kind of promotion that comes from God, not people?

Where do you see yourself in 6 months as it relates to this chapter's theme?

Where do you see yourself in 1 year as it relates to this chapter's theme?

CHAPTER 12

Leadership, Influence, the Call to Serve

Leadership in the kingdom is not about position. It is not about titles, platforms, or recognition. Leadership begins with responsibility — the willingness to carry what God places in your hands and to steward it with humility, integrity, and faith. Leadership is not something you wait to be given; it is something you grow into through service.

Jesus made this clear when He said, "Whoever wants to become great among you must be your servant" (Matthew 20:26). In the kingdom, greatness is measured by service. Influence is measured by faithfulness. Leadership is measured by character. The world promotes people based on visibility; God promotes people based on humility.

Leadership begins with influence. Influence is not loud. It is not forceful. It is not demanding. Influence is the quiet strength of a life lived with consistency. It is the impact of integrity. It is the weight of character. People follow leaders they trust, not leaders who talk the most. Influence is earned long before it is recognized.

Leadership also begins with stewardship. God gives every believer gifts, opportunities, relationships, and responsibilities. How you steward what you have determines what God can entrust to you next. Luke 16:10 teaches that,

"whoever is faithful with little will be faithful with much." *(KJV)*

Faithfulness is the foundation of leadership. It is the training ground for influence. Leadership requires humility. Humility is not weakness; it is strength under control. It is the ability to lead without needing attention. It is the ability to serve without needing applause. It is the ability to influence without needing credit. Humility keeps leadership pure. It keeps influence grounded. It keeps the heart aligned with God.

Leadership also requires courage. Courage is not the absence of fear; it is the willingness to act in spite of it. Leaders step forward when others hesitate. They speak truth when silence feels safer. They take responsibility when others avoid it. Courage is the backbone of leadership. It is what allows leaders to stand firm when pressure rises.

Leadership requires vision. Vision is the ability to see beyond the present moment. It is the ability to recognize potential where others see problems. It is the ability to see what God is doing even when circumstances seem unclear. Vision lifts people. Vision guides decisions. Vision creates direction. Without vision, leadership becomes maintenance instead of movement.

Leadership also requires compassion. Jesus led with compassion. He saw people, not crowds. He noticed needs, not numbers. He responded to individuals, not statistics. Compassion is what keeps leadership human. It keeps influence relational. It keeps ministry grounded in love. Without compassion, leadership becomes mechanical. With compassion, leadership becomes transformative.

Leadership requires wisdom. Wisdom is the ability to discern the right action at the right time for the right reason. Wisdom protects leaders from impulsive decisions, unnecessary conflicts, and avoidable mistakes. James 1:5 teaches that God gives wisdom generously to those who ask,

5 Do any of you need wisdom? Ask God for it. He is generous and enjoys giving to everyone. So, he will give you wisdom. (ERV)

Leaders who seek wisdom lead with clarity, stability, and peace. Leadership requires servanthood. Jesus washed the disciples' feet — not because He had to, but because He wanted to show them what leadership looks like. Servanthood is not a task; it is a posture. It is the willingness to do what others overlook. It is the willingness to lift others higher. It is the willingness to lead by example, not by demand.

Now, you are the mentor, the example. If you do not lead with integrity, who will? If you do not influence your environment with godly character, who will? If you do not serve with humility, who will? If you do not carry God's heart into your sphere, who will? Leadership is not someone else's assignment. It is yours. It is part of your identity. It is part of your calling. It is part of your purpose.

Now is the time to lead. Now is the time to influence. Now is the time to serve. Now is the time to step into the responsibility God has placed before you. Leadership is not about waiting for permission. It is about responding to God's invitation. It is about recognizing that your life carries weight. Your presence carries influence. Your obedience carries impact. You are not leading alone. God is with you. God is guiding you. God is shaping you. God is preparing you. Leadership is not a destination — it is a journey. A journey of service. A journey of growth. A journey of faithfulness and you are already on that path.

Leadership, Influence, and the Call to Serve

A lot of people hesitate to see themselves as leaders because they assume leadership requires a title, a platform, or a certain personality. They think leadership is something that happens once someone else recognizes them. But leadership in the kingdom has never started with visibility. It starts with responsibility — the quiet, consistent choice to steward what's already in your hands with humility and integrity. If you've ever felt the weight of responsibility before you felt the weight of recognition, that's usually the first sign that leadership is already forming in you.

You might be someone who serves faithfully but feels unseen. You might be someone who influences people without realizing it. Or maybe you've been waiting for permission to step into something you already feel stirring inside you. But leadership isn't granted by people — it's grown through character. Influence isn't loud or demanding. It's earned through consistency, honesty, and the kind of life that people trust. And if you've ever wondered whether your quiet faithfulness matters, it does. It's shaping you more than you realize.

Jesus made leadership simple: greatness looks like serving. Not serving to be noticed. Not serving to climb. Serving because your heart is aligned with God's. When you carry that posture, people begin to feel the weight of your life — not because you're trying to lead them, but because your integrity gives them something steady to follow. Leadership is not about being in front. It's about being someone worth following.

What I now know: you don't need a title to lead. You don't need a spotlight to have influence. You don't need a position to carry weight. What you need is the willingness to serve with humility, to live with integrity, and to let God shape your character in the hidden places. Leadership is not something you wait for — it's something you grow into, one act of faithfulness at a time. And before you move forward, take a moment to picture your own development. If you embraced the call to serve with greater intentionality, where could you realistically see yourself in six months when it comes to influence, consistency, and the way others experience your leadership? And if you continued to grow in humility and integrity, where could you see yourself in one year in terms of the kind of leader you're becoming — not by title, but by character?

Where do you see yourself in 6 months as it relates to this chapter's theme?

Where do you see yourself in 1 year as it relates to this chapter's theme?

CHAPTER 13

Legacy, Generosity, and Kingdom Impact

There comes a moment in every believer's journey when God shifts the conversation from understanding to movement. Up to this point, He has been forming your foundation — shaping your identity, strengthening your faith, and clarifying your calling. But now, He begins to speak with a different tone. It is the tone of invitation mixed with urgency, the tone of a Father who knows you are ready for more than you realize. This chapter is about recognizing that shift and responding to it with confidence, clarity, and obedience.

You are not stepping into something unfamiliar — you are stepping into what God has been preparing you for all along. The prophetic edge of this chapter is not meant to overwhelm you; it is meant to awaken you. It is meant to remind you that God does not call you into motion without first equipping you for it. As you read, allow the Holy Spirit to highlight the areas where He is already stirring you forward. This is not theory. This is training. This is preparation. This is the moment where your faith begins to take shape in real movement.

Legacy doesn't begin when your life ends. Legacy begins the moment you decide your life is not just about you. This is where everything shifts. Because legacy is not built in someday. Legacy is built on daily decisions.

In quiet obedience. In unseen faithfulness. In the choices you make when no one is watching. Legacy is not a future concept — it is a present posture.

Here's the truth most people never realize: You are already building a legacy. The question is whether it's intentional or accidental. Legacy is the echo of your life. It's the imprint you leave on people. It's the faith you pass down. It's the generosity you sow. It's the courage you model. It's the obedience you live out. Legacy is not measured in accomplishments. It's measured in impact and impact always begins with generosity.

Generosity is not about money — it's about posture. It's about living open-handed. It's about recognizing that everything you have came from God, and everything you give returns to Him. Generosity breaks fear. Generosity breaks scarcity. Generosity breaks self-preservation. Generosity opens the door for God to move through you in ways you never imagined. Because generosity is not loss — it is multiplication.

Scripture teaches in Ecclesiastes 11:1, that when you cast your bread upon the waters, it returns after many days:

11 Do good wherever you go. [a] After a while, the good you do will come back to you. (ERV)

That's not poetry. That's principle. That's kingdom economics. That's how God turns obedience into impact.

Allow me to mentor you on the part most believers miss: Generosity is one of the fastest ways to shift your spiritual authority. Why? Because generosity aligns your heart with God's heart. God so loved the world that He gave. Giving is not something God does — it is who He is. When you give, you reflect Him. When you sow, you partner with Him. When you bless others, you carry His nature into the world. I don't hear an Amen from you. Generosity is not about the size of the gift. It's about the size of the obedience.

Some of the greatest kingdom impact comes from the smallest acts of faithfulness.

A conversation

A prayer

A meal

A moment of encouragement

A seed sown quietly

A sacrifice no one else sees

Heaven sees it. Heaven records it. Heaven multiplies it. Legacy is built one seed at a time. Here's where the urgency rises:

Your life is shaping someone else's faith

Someone is watching how you respond to pressure

Someone is learning from how you handle conflict

Someone is being strengthened by your consistency

Someone is being encouraged by your courage

Someone is being lifted by your generosity

You are influencing people you don't even realize you're influencing. This is why the enemy fights you so hard. Not because of who you are today — but because of who you are becoming. Because of the people your life will touch. Because of the legacy your obedience will build. Legacy is not about being remembered. Legacy is about making sure God is revealed. This is why I'm pleading with you, If Not You, Who? If you don't build a legacy of faith, who will? If you don't model generosity, who will? If you don't carry kingdom impact into your sphere, who will? If you don't step into your assignment, who will?

Legacy is not waiting for someone else. Legacy is waiting for you. I'm begging you to consider this: If Not Now, When? Will you start sowing intentionally? Will you start living generously? Will you start building what God placed in your heart? Will you start walking in the impact God designed for you? Remember, legacy is not built in the future, legacy is built in the now. This is because your life is bigger than your lifetime and your obedience to the Lord will outlive you. Your generosity will ripple into generations. Your faith will become someone else's foundation.

This is your moment. This is your season. This is your assignment, but they are not for you, they are for someone else! Build the legacy heaven wrote for you and live generously. Sow boldly. Impact deeply. The kingdom is waiting for what only you can release.

Legacy, Generosity, and Kingdom Impact

There comes a point in your walk with God where the conversation shifts. It's no longer just about understanding who you are or discovering what you're called to do. It becomes about movement — real, tangible movement. If you've been sensing that shift, it's because God has already been preparing you for it. Everything He's been forming in you — identity, faith, clarity, responsibility — has been leading to this moment where what you believe starts to take shape in how you live.

You might feel the tension of transition. You might feel the weight of responsibility settling in a new way. Or maybe you're realizing that the things God has been stirring in you are no longer ideas — they're invitations. That's not pressure. That's readiness. God never calls you into motion without equipping you first. If something in you feels like it's time to step forward, that's because the foundation has already been laid.

Legacy begins long before anyone remembers your name. It begins the moment you decide your life is not just about you. It begins when generosity becomes natural, when obedience becomes instinctive, when impact becomes intentional. Legacy isn't built in dramatic moments — it's built on daily decisions. It's built in the quiet choices no one sees, the sacrifices no one applauds, and the faithfulness that feels ordinary.

Where do you see yourself in 6 months as it relates to this chapter's theme?

Where do you see yourself in 1 year as it relates to this chapter's theme?

CHAPTER 14

Walking Out Your Calling: A Life of Faith and Obedience

Leadership in the Kingdom is never accidental. It is always the result of formation, surrender, and intentional growth. Everything you have walked through in the previous chapters has been preparing you for this moment — the moment where calling becomes responsibility, and responsibility becomes influence. This responsibility is designed to bring clarity to your assignment and confidence to your leadership. You are not stepping into leadership alone; you are stepping into it with the wisdom, presence, and guidance of the Holy Spirit.

Allow yourself to see leadership not as a title, but as a stewardship. God entrusts influence to those who have allowed Him to shape their character and as you become more influential, these lessons on mentorship will help you recognize the areas where God is strengthening your voice, refining your decisions, and expanding your capacity. You are being positioned for impact — not by accident, but by design. Let these words anchor you, steady you, and prepare you for the weight of what God is placing in your hands. They are written with sincerity of heart because we might not always know what to do, but we published this book because we know what not to do.

Calling is not fulfilled in inspiration. Calling is fulfilled in obedience. You do not step into purpose by emotion, excitement, mental assent or intention. You step into purpose by action — consistent, deliberate, faith-driven action. This is the point where understanding must become movement. Where revelation must become responsibility. Where identity must become expression. You have learned enough. You have grown enough. You have been prepared long enough. Now you must walk.

Walking out your calling requires clarity. Clarity about who you are. Clarity about what God has spoken. Clarity about what matters most in this season. Why? Great question.... Because clarity eliminates distraction. Clarity exposes excuses. Clarity creates direction. You cannot walk confidently when you are unclear internally. You cannot move forward while negotiating with doubt. You cannot fulfill your assignment while entertaining alternatives. Your calling requires a decision — a firm, settled, internal yes. You owe it to both your mentors and those who you mentor.

Walking out your calling also requires discipline. Discipline is the structure that protects destiny. Discipline is the boundary that keeps you aligned. Discipline is the daily choice that builds long-term impact. You cannot drift into purpose. You cannot stumble into obedience. You cannot casually arrive at destiny. Purpose is pursued, obedience is practiced and calling is cultivated. Walking out your calling requires courage. Courage to begin.

Courage to continue. Courage to stand when others sit. Courage to speak when silence feels safer. Courage to obey when obedience costs you something. Courage is not emotional intensity. Courage is sustained conviction.

Walking out your calling requires faith. Faith that God is with you. Faith that God is guiding you. Faith that God is strengthening you. Faith that God is opening the right doors and closing the wrong ones. Faith is not a feeling — it is a posture. Faith is not certainty — it is trust. Faith is not comfort — it is confidence in God's character.

Walking out your call requires alignment. Alignment with God's voice. Alignment with God's timing. Alignment with God's priorities. Misalignment creates delays. Alignment creates acceleration.

Walking out your call requires accountability. You need people who sharpen you. People who challenge you. People who remind you of what God said. People who refuse to let you shrink back. Isolation weakens calling. Community strengthens it.

Walking out your call requires endurance. Not every season will be easy. Not every assignment will be comfortable. Not every step will be celebrated, but endurance produces maturity. Endurance produces resilience. Endurance produces authority.

Walking out your calling requires obedience. Obedience when it makes sense and obedience when it doesn't. Obedience when it costs you. Obedience when it stretches you. Obedience when it separates you. Obedience is the currency of calling. Obedience is the proof of faith. Obedience is the pathway to impact.

We leave you with this final thought to consider: If you do not walk out your calling, who will step into the space God designed for you? If you do not obey, who will carry the assignment tied to your name? If you do not move, who will reach the people connected to your obedience? If you do not rise, who will fill the gap your life was meant to fill? Your call is not transferable. Your assignment is not replaceable. Your purpose is not optional.

Will you begin? Will you obey fully? Will you stop delaying what God has already confirmed? Will you step into the life heaven has been preparing you for?

Well Dear believer, we know that we know that you will. Calling is not activated in the future. Calling is activated in the present. This is your moment. As you place this book down and ingest these mentorship moments together, remember that this is your season. This is your responsibility. Walk with clarity. Walk with courage. Walk with conviction. Walk with faith. Walk with obedience. Walk out your calling — boldly, consistently, and without apology.

Walking Out Your Calling: A Life of Faith and Obedience

You might feel the weight of this shift. You might feel the tension between who you've been and who you're becoming. Or maybe you're realizing that obedience is no longer optional — it's the natural next step. That's not pressure. That's maturity. God doesn't call you into leadership accidentally. He calls you because He has already been shaping your character, strengthening your resolve, and preparing your heart to carry what He's placing in your hands.

Walking out your calling isn't about hype. It isn't about excitement. It isn't about waiting for the perfect moment. It's about choosing to act on what God has already spoken. It's about trusting His voice more than your hesitation. It's about letting obedience become the rhythm of your life, not just the response to a spiritual moment. If you've ever wondered whether you're capable of this, remember: God doesn't ask you to walk alone. He leads. He steadies. He strengthens. He guides. He uses people to help people. God bless you on Your journey Today!

Where do you see yourself in 6 months as it relates to this chapter's theme?

Where do you see yourself in 1 year as it relates to this chapter's theme?

85